1

The Complete Book Of Softball Drills

The Complete Book Of Softball Drills

By Gary LeLand

ISBN-13: 9781499569254

ISBN-10: 1499569254

Printed in the United States of America

Table Of Contents

Preface

I first became involved with softball at the YMCA in Arlington, Texas. My two daughters ages eight and nine wanted to add yet another sport to their already busy schedule. We played ten games in our first season, and won the YMCA championship.

When the season ended the coach asked all the parents for a volunteer. She felt she needed someone to take over the team who knew more about the game. I reluctantly volunteered after no one else did. Little did I know that moment would change my life forever.

I quickly moved my team from slowpitch to fastpitch. We then transitioned from a recreational to a select league.

By the time the team was 14 and under we claimed out first win in the Texas USSSA State Tournament. The following year we repeated by winning the Texas USSSA 15 and Under State Tournament. After two consecutive state wins we then placed 5th and 4th in different national events.

I now operate a full time business dedicated to fastpitch softball. I currently publish "The Fastpitch Softball Magazine" a magazine exclusively featuring fastpitch softball. I own and operate a retail softball store in Texas SoftballJunk.com, and yes it has a website. I even have a website Fastpitch.TV that has numerous free training videos to view, and blogs.

I am currently the USSSA State director for Fastpitch Softball in Texas.

I have also invented and created many training aids specifically for fastpitch softball.

One of the things I remember when first starting was my passion to learn new information. I was dedicated to find information anywhere I could.

It was through all my experiences and knowledge I decided to write this book. My goal was to make a great guide for a parent wanting to improve the skills of their daughter or their team. The drills used in this book were used by my team, friends, and other coaches. I truly believe you will find the drills to be helpful and beneficial.

Gary LeLand

Catching Drills

Box Jumps

This drill is an effective way to gain strength for quick movements, speed, and endurance.

This drill will require a 2 foot high box that is sturdy enough for you to jump on

The catcher will stand behind the box and another player will stand 2 feet in front of the box with a ball.

The player will toss the ball high and directly above the box.

When the player releases the box the catcher explodes up to land on top of the box and catches the ball.

Make 10 jumps and then rotate.

Drop Third Out – Catchers Drills

This drill is a great way to ensure that when a drop third strike occurs in a game that the catcher know what to do and can execute the play efficiently.

Create a game like situation when the batter swings and the ball drops to the dirt first.

The batter will take off to first base and the catcher must find the ball and throw the ball to first base before the batter reaches the bag.

Catcher Observations

This drill is an effective way to encourage catchers to make their own observations and gain experience in calling pitches that will benefit the team.

The coach will give all of the catchers the task of observing a select few of their teammates when they are batting without them knowing.

At the end of practice the coach will take note of each of the catcher's observations.

The catchers will then meet with the coach together and discuss what would be the best approach to dealing with the batters that were observed in a game situation.

Do this once a week and chance the batters to be observed each week.

Backing Up the Throw

This drill is great for working on plays that often occur in games as well as building a catchers value and skills in the sport.

When there are no runners on base and the play is being made at home plate the catcher should always be ready to back up the throw to 1st base.

As soon as the hit is made the catcher should judge where the ball will be stopped and if that ball is going to be thrown to first base then the catcher should flip off her mask and head over to first base just in the case that a wild throw is made.

Too often do teams get an extra base from wild throws?

The catcher should always make backing up throws to 1st base a habit in those situations.

Wall Sits

This is a great, classic exercise to build muscle strength in the lower body and increase endurance.

The catcher can either do this with or without gear. (With gear for more advanced players)

Lean against a wall or fence forming a 90 degree angle at your knees

Hold this position until you feel a burning sensation in your legs and then try to hold for another 15 seconds.

The 5 x 5

This drill is great conditioning for a catcher while practicing basic catching skills

The coach will stand about 5-10 feet in front of home plate and the catcher will wear full gear and take his/her stance behind the plate.

The coach will throw the first 5 balls in the dirt and the catcher will have to block them

The coach will throw the next 5 balls far out to the sides and the catcher will have to move and block the balls only with his/her body

The coach will throw the next 5 balls high and the catcher will have to pop up to catch them.

The coach will throw the next 5 balls at random

The coach will finish with throwing pop-ups right after one of the balls is caught.

This drill will be great to do with 2-3 catchers take their turn at the drill one of the catchers can help shag balls and the other can take a small break before going through the drill again.

The Grip Drill

This drill will break the habit of a catcher always dropping to their knees when throwing back to the pitcher.

The catcher will be in full gear and squat into the catching position and throw back with remaining mostly in the same position.

This is a difficult habit to break but a catcher must not be in the habit of dropping to their knees when runners are on base or else the runners will see that as lazy and attempt to steal more often.

Hip Exercise

This drill is great for warm-ups to avoid injury and build strength in the lower body

Place 2 sturdy boxes about 1 foot high shoulder width apart.

The player will stand between the 2 boxes and lift his/her right leg and step on the box to the right

Then back to the center

Then the player will lift his/her left leg and step onto the box to the left.

Repeat this drill until you reach 20 steps

Pitcher Throwback

This drill will break the habit of a catcher always dropping to their knees when throwing back to the pitcher.

The catcher will be in full gear and squat into the catching position and throw back with remaining mostly in the same position.

This is a difficult habit to break but a catcher must not be in the habit of dropping to their knees when runners are on base or else the runners will see that as lazy and attempt to steal more often.

Catcher Crossfire

This drill is great conditioning for a catcher as well as accuracy in throwing.

The catcher takes their stance behind the plate. The pitcher, third, and first baseman will take their position half way from their base and home plate.

This drill will utilize 2 balls

The balls begin with the pitcher and the first baseman.

The ball will be lightly pitched to the catcher and the catcher will pop up and lightly throw to the 3rd baseman while the first baseman throws the ball to the pitcher and continues the drill.

This is fast paced and will cause the catcher to become tired.

Begin with 10 throws and then increase by even increments to build endurance. Make sure to take breaks in between!

Relay to the Catcher

This drill is an effective way to practice players hitting the appropriate cut-off when a ball is hit to the outfield.

Have all infielders in their positions and have 6-8 outfielders spread out evenly 10 feet in front of the outfield fence.

The coach will give a game situation and then call out one of the players in the outfield.

The catcher must direct the girls to line up the cut-off throw as straight as possible to make the play. (The catcher makes the directions because she has the best view of the entire field)

This will give the catcher experience and confidence to make quick decisions in game situations.

Catcher Conditioning

This drill is an effective way to build muscle and speed for catchers.

The catcher will be in full gear, without a glove.

The catcher will take his/her stance with both hands behind their back.

In a very fast paced motions the catcher will drop the right knee, then the left knee, pick up the right knee, and then pick up the left knee, and be back in his/her catching stance.

The catcher should not squat any higher than the position that they originally started at.

This drill is quick and should begin with about 10 knee drops and then slowly build up to more at a time.

The Pick Off

This drill is an advanced alternative to picking off the runner leading off at first base.

This drill will require all infield except for the third baseman, and one base runner.

The pitcher will pitch the ball and the shortstop will shift towards second base (In case the runner decides to steal)

The catcher shoots the ball to the second baseman, either preventing the runner from stealing or tagging the runner as she attempts to steal.

With more advanced teams the second baseman will either throw back to first for the tag on the dive back, throw to second for the tag on the steal, or move to tag the runner herself.

Repeat this drill with live runners to perfect it. This will surprise other teams, as it is not a typical drill for picking off the runner.

Quick Corners

This drill will aid the catcher in accuracy to picking off runners at 1st and 3rd

The catcher will be in full gear behind the plate. One coach/player will be about 5 feet in front of home plate with a bucket of balls, and one player at 1st and 3rd.

The coach will toss the balls to the catcher who will throw to 1st and 3rd, alternating between the two until the bucket is empty.

This drill is quick with little time for the catcher to reset in between.

The catcher will become fatigued.

Catching Endurance

This drill will build strength and endurance for a catcher

The catcher will wear her full gear for this drill.

Place 5 balls in a semi-circle in front of the plate.

The catcher will begin a couple of feet behind home plate and complete a series of 3 up-downs, 5 jumping jacks, 2 pushups and then run to the ball furthest to the right and throw it to the coach at 2nd base.

Continue this until the balls are gone and take a break

Repeat. This drill is quick and will be exhausting, but will build the catchers strength, endurance, and stamina for long games and days of high heat.

Runners Running

This drill is a fun and competitive way to experience catchers in fielding bunts.

With runners standing at home and first base, the coach (who is behind the catcher) will toss the ball over the catchers shoulder simulating a bunt,

The catcher fields the bunt, decides which runner to throw out, and makes the throw.

One point goes to defense if the runner is thrown out at first and two points if the runner is thrown out at second.

Offense earns one point for reaching second safely and one-half point for reaching first safely. Whichever team earns five points first, wins!

Shadow Drill

This drill is great for younger and older catchers to maintain being in excellent shape especially for warm weather and a long season that can take its toll on a catcher.

Two catchers will begin in full gear facing each other.

One catcher will begin as the leader and simulate typical catching motions(squatting, dropping to the knees for a wild pitch, catching the pitch and throwing down a runner) while the other catcher "shadows" all of the motions.

After about three minutes take a small break and have the other catcher be the leader.

Backstop Drill

This drill is an effective way to have the catchers work on retrieving balls near the backstop and making the play at the plate. This also helps to alleviate some of the pitcher's anxieties about making the play on the runner stealing home.

Dump a bucket of balls along the backstop behind the catcher.

The catcher will begin in his/her usual stance and the pitcher waits just inside the pitching circle.

On "GO" the catcher mist turn around, go for the ball, look quickly, and backhand the ball to the pitcher running in. The pitcher works on fielding the ball and making the tag.

Continue this drill until the catcher is able to accurately place the ball at the plate on repeated tries and then add a runner attempting to steal home.

Soft Hands

This drill teaches the catcher to catch the ball properly

You will need tennis balls or safety balls and have the catcher take his/her stance behind the plate without a glove.

The coach or a partner throws the tennis balls or the safety balls close to the strike zone.

The catcher attempts to catch every pitch with the proper hand position and then drops the ball in front of her.

The person pitching should have a bucket or bag of balls to throw as quickly as the catcher can handle them.

Duck Walks

This drill is simple but provides the best results for a catcher's agility, speed, mobility, strength, and endurance.

The catcher must be in full gear

Have the catcher remain in her stance and walk (Duck walk) around the bases.

This is very challenging and tiring, but must be done correctly for the best results

Make sure that the catcher does not raise herself to a certain height and use her arms for support on her knees or hips.

Begin with short distances and then work up to all of the bases so long as the movements are correct when made.

Foul Agility

This drill provides work on a catcher's agility and movement to get to a foul ball.

This drill requires a catcher and a person to toss the balls.

The catcher will lay flat on her stomach behind home plate in full gear.

The partner will yell "Foul" and toss the ball up and in foul territory

The catcher will quickly scramble to find and catch the ball.

Pop-Up

This drill is an effective way to get your catcher used to catching pop up's behind the plate.

Begin with the catcher in a crouched position behind the plate.

The coach will use a tennis racket and a tennis ball and hit one straight in the air and give the command to find and catch the ball.

The tennis balls are bouncy, therefor the catch must be made with 2 hands.

For advanced catchers, once one ball is hit and the catcher finds it to catch hit another for him/her to get to immediately after.

Shin Guard Shuffle

This drill focuses on getting acquainted with the equipment, footwork, hand-eye coordination, endurance and quickness. Softball Catchers must develop themselves physically aside from just developing skills.

This drill has 2 catchers in full gear

The two catchers will be facing each other about 4' apart

On the command of the coach the catchers will shuffle in a circle and wait for the coach's next command

The coach's commands include:

"Left": Rotate Left

"Right": Rotate Right

"Up": Simulate a Pop Up

"Down": Simulate a block in the dirt

"Throw": Simulate a throw to second

"Push-Up": Do an actual Push-Up

"Sit-Up": Do an actual Sit-Up

"Jog": Jog in place

Upper Body Warm-Up

This drill will provide muscle memory for catchers to remember to bring the ball and glove to their ear when approaching a throw for optimum power and speed.

Throwing with a partner works best for this drill.

Begin standing about 40' to 60' apart with toes facing the player's partner.

Throw the ball to your partner without moving your feet, rotating your upper body and lining up your shoulders with your target and throw.

When the ball is received the partner will drive the ball to the bare hand back and up to the right ear and then proceed to throw as explained before.

Framing

This drill will provide experience in perfecting framing pitches in games.

Start by having the catcher, in full gear, set up behind the plate.

The coach will begin to throw softballs (balls, strikes, outside, inside)

Whatever the pitch may be have the catcher attempt to rotate and move their glove in such a way that it will appear to be a strike to the umpire.

Movements should not be over-the-top as to avoid obvious framing.

Catching Wall Drill

This drill is designed to improve a catchers blocking skills as well as overall catching mechanics.

While in full catching gear have the catcher face a wall and stand about 5 to 6 feet from it.

Have the coach or another player stand behind the catcher

The coach or player will throw softballs, tennis balls, or any other balls that you prefer against the wall

As soon as the ball hits the wall the catcher will move to where the ball is and drop to his/her knees to block the ball from getting past him/her. (Glove is optional, but if the catcher catches the ball then make sure that it is with his/her glove hand).

Sign System

This exercise is to remind catchers of the basic rules of pitching signs and give a few helpful hints to better the communication between the catcher and the pitcher.

First, finger movements should be slow and controlled. Rushing the signs will not allow the pitcher to clearly read the signs.

When making a sign the catcher's hand should be placed back against the cup or groin and the fingers should always be pointing down.

Make sure that the fingers are not too low so that the on-deck hitter or individuals behind the catcher cannot see the signs.

Close off both knees and keep them facing towards the pitcher. If knees are open, then the coaches in the coaching box may be able to see your signs and relay them to the hitter. (There is nothing wrong with stealing signs if the catcher is doing a poor job)

Have as little hand movement as possible. Do not give away pitches with loud arm or hand movements.

The key is to move slow, deliberate, and subtly.

Practicing this with just the pitcher and catcher or in front of a mirror is very beneficial.

Bounce at Plate

This drill is an effective way to get a catcher used to blocking the ball from getting past them.

Set up a pitching machine at the pitcher's mound and shoot balls into the ground just behind home plate and in front of home plate.

The catcher must be in full gear and catch the balls so that they do not go behind her.

After becoming comfortable blocking the ball with using a glove, tie the catcher's hands behind her back and throw sponge balls. (Not regular balls) This version will improve movement to the ball.

Drawing Cross

This drill will provide muscle memory and strength training for catchers when they receive a pitch.

Begin by drawing a cross in front of the catcher while he/she is in position behind the plate. Crouching down on one of the lines, a catcher should be able to pop-up and land on the other line that crosses it.

Continue repeating the pop up motion and remember that when a catcher throws, their hand should always be brought up to their ear and then throw.

Combining the "pop-up" and the proper throw will gain speed on the throw down to second.

Throwing Footwork

This drill exercises proper foot work and anticipating steals from the other team.

This will require 2 players. One catching and one throwing.

The catcher will assume her stance as if there is a runner on first base and the pitcher will throw the ball around the strike zone.

Once the ball is caught the catcher should quickly execute the proper footwork to get to the throwing position.

This is just a foot work drill, so once the proper throwing position is reached then the catcher should pause with the ball in her throwing hand and flip the ball back to the pitcher.

Repeat about ten to twelve times. Take a break and repeat on the other side.

Reaction

Have the catcher, in full gear, crouch four feet away from a wall. The coach/player stands two feet behind the catcher and throws the ball over the head of the catcher and at the wall. The catcher can not see the throw and must react to where it rebounds off of the wall.

Insist on good side to side movement, containing the ball with the shoulders, and staying square behind the ball. As the catchers get more proficient at this drill, vary the speed and angles at which the ball comes off of the wall.

This drill helps the catcher develop quickness and a good response time.

Throw Down

This drill will exercise a catcher's ability to field a ball and throw it to any position needed.

Lay five to six balls in a semi-circle in front of a fully dressed catcher. From her stance have him/her retrieve one ball and throw it down, using proper throwing techniques, then return to her stance.

Continue drill until he/she has thrown all of the balls. Time him/her for fun and make sure to emphasize accuracy.

This drill will build confidence and trust between the players.

This drill can be incorporated with different positions and players.

Slide to Speed

This drill will develop strength and speed in a catcher's ability to move to block the ball.

With the catcher behind the plate in full gear have the coach or pitcher pitch or throw the balls to both sides of the catcher.

This is most effective with 50 balls at a time and completed once before and after practice.

The drill is tiring because you do not have time to get up and walk back to the plate.

Hula

This drill focuses on accuracy and helps form a connection between catcher and pitcher.

This will require the catcher, pitcher, coach, a third player, several softballs, and a hula hoop.

Catcher and pitcher are in their positions, the third player is on second, and the coach stands between second base and the pitching circle holding the hula hoop directly in the line of play.

The catcher will throw a softball through the hula hoop to the player standing at second base.

For added challenge and better game simulation, the pitcher stands in the pitching circle and ducks when he/she sees the catcher throw.

Trash Can

This drill focuses on a catcher's accuracy and speed.

For this drill you will need a very large plastic trash can, and 10 balls.

Lay the trash can down to the right of second base with the open top facing directly towards home plate.

The catcher will then proceed to throw 10 balls into the trash can.

Now move the trash can slightly to the right of third base with the open top facing home plate again. Repeat the drill.

Paddles

This drill focuses on coordination, speed and may also ease nerves concerning incoming pitches.

This drill requires the catcher, a second player or coach, and two wooden paddles with ropes.

The catcher will crouch in full gear, with the wooden paddles tied to his/her hands instead of gloves. Be sure the catcher has a wall behind him/her.

The second player/coach will repeatedly throw balls to the ground directly in front of the catcher so that the catcher may block the balls with the paddles on his/her hands.

Fielding Drills

Cross Fielding

This drill is an effective way to push players to exhaustion and still promote proper fielding.

Two coaches will be set up at home plate to hit fungo to one player at 2nd and the other coach to hit to one player at short stop. There should be one player at third and first to catch balls as well.

The Coaches will hit and entire bucket of balls to the players at second base and short stop.

The second baseman will field the ball and throw to 3rd base. The short stop will field the ball and throw to the first baseman.

The fielders will become fatigued, but then for encouragement make it into a competition to see how many balls that a player can correctly field and throw without error.

When finished the first and third baseman will exchange buckets with the coaches and proceed to the back of the 2nd or short-stop line and the fielders will rotate to the base they threw too.

Get Dirty

This drill will aid players in becoming accustomed to the motions of diving.

Have all of the player's partner up with one softball per group.

Begin this drill in outfield first

The players will drop to their knees, facing each other about 10 feet apart.

One player will roll the balls and one will receive.

The player with the ball will roll it about 4 feet to the right or the left of their partner.

The player receiving the ball will lay out and stop the ball before it goes past.

After 10 dives, switch. As the players become more comfortable with the motions roll the balls faster and for infielders have those players move to the dirt.

Star Fielding

This drill will boost a players stamina and while working on foot work and accuracy.

Set up the infield with a first baseman, short stop, third baseman, and a catcher to feed balls to the coach who is hitting fungo.

The coach will hit the ball to the short stop, who will then use proper foot work to tag 2nd base and throw to the third baseman.

The third baseman will catch the ball, tag third and then throw to first.

The first baseman will catch the ball, tag first base, and then throw the ball back to the catcher.

Continue the drill about 5-6 times without error and then switch the players.

This drill is quick and will only allow the players a few seconds of rest in between fielding the ball and resetting for the next one.

Turning 2

This drill is an effective way to practice making a double play.

Have the coach as the hitter and the entire infield in position.

The coach will hit the ball at random and the situation will always be to get the imaginary runner out at second and then turn the double play at first.

When infield preforms up to par then add in a base runner at first to add pressure to the defense to make the play.

Ground Ball Game

This drill will promote fun competition between the players on the team.

All of the players will line up behind third base.

The first player will step out about 8 – 9 steps to the right of the plate.

The coach will then hit a ground ball to the player.

Once all of the players have gotten one ground ball then the hits will become harder and have more range in the direction that they are going.

One a player misses the ball then they are out

The last player standing is the winner.

Play this at the end of every practice or once a week with the incentive that at the end of the month, or season, that the player that has won the most gets a gift card or something of that nature.

Palm

This drill develops the basic mechanics of fielding a ball and transitioning into a throwing position.

Begin with three or four players with their gloves off, about 15' away from the thrower.

The players are in a fielding position as if they are about to receive the ball.

With the palm of the glove hand facing down and fingers spread toss the ball to the player.

The goal is to tap the ball straight down to the ground with the palm of the glove hand.

When progressing to the next step introduce the throwing hand with literally having the player tap the ball into the throwing hand, not catching the ball, but tapping the ball into the throwing hand.

There should be two soft sounds: the first is the ball hitting the glove hand, and the second is the ball falling into the throwing hand.

Progress again to the next step of doing the same as before but add the foot work to get into a throwing position.

Statue

This drill helps the coaches evaluate a players motions when throwing as well as provides a fun game for everyone while focusing on proper mechanics.

Begin with having the players throw balls back and forth between one another.

At random, call out "statue!" and all of the players must become statues in their throwing position.

The coach will check for proper position and grip.

The best "Statue" wins that round.

Red Rover

This drill is a fun and competitive way to work on quick feet and fielding ground balls.

Make 2 teams and set up 2 sets of cones approximately 15'-20' apart.

Spread the 2 team out evenly between the cones and have the teams facing each other.

Give one team the ball and have them begin throwing grounders at the opposing team. If a grounder gets through the opposing line then the player who missed the ball is out.

If 2 or more players go for the ball and miss then the opposing team chooses who is out!

Using a Bucket of Ballss

This is a great drill for infielders or even outfielders to make the cut-off throw or get the ball to home plate as quickly and accurately as possible.

Take a bucket of balls and scatter the balls around about 10 feet behind where shortstop would normally be. (The same can be done for second base as well.

Have the short stop turn around and field one of the balls and take the throw to home plate. (Use a bucket at home plate if there is not another player to catch.

For outfielders scatter the balls around the middle of the outfield and have them charge the ball and throw to the cut off or to home plate.

Throwing Form

This drill will help develop proper form when throwing.

Have someone standing about 5 feet directly behind the player.

The thrower should take a ball and, from the hand in glove position (as if the ball were just fielded), separate the hands with the ball hand swinging first down, then back and up until her throwing arm bicep is parallel with the ground and she has a 90 degree angle with her forearm pointing up and the ball facing backwards.

Looking at this motion from the third base side, the ball hand starts at 9 o'clock, swings down to 6 o'clock then up to 12 o'clock (if the player is a right handed thrower). If the ball is released at about 3 o'clock and the player's form is correct, the ball should be easily caught by the person standing behind her. If the ball goes to the left or right of the catcher, she is not using a proper path for her arm.

When the player has the proper arm motion, have her go into your throwing motion instead of releasing the ball. She should stride with her lead foot and follow through.

That Game

This drill/game is a great team bonding tool, it is fun, and also allows the practice of the basic fundamentals of the game.

Split the players into 3 teams. The game works well with 12 girls (3 teams of 4 players) and 2 coaches. One team goes to the outfield, one team plays the infield and the other team is up to bat.

One coach pitches and one catches. If there is only one coach, use a tee and have the coach play catcher. Once the ball has been hit, the team who touches the ball first has to pass the ball under their legs until it has been touched by every girl on their team. The last girl has to throw the ball to the catcher before the batter/runner makes it home. The throw home has to be a good throw and the coach receiving the throw home can stand on home plate and can stretch to catch the ball. However, he can't leave the plate.

If the ball arrives before the runner then the home team has one out. After three outs, the players rotate – the team at bat goes to outfield, the outfield team goes to infield, and the infield team goes to bat. The catch is that the pitcher can pitch as soon as a batter is up to the plate with a helmet on, so if a girls' team was just at bat, she had better be running to position herself in the outfield.

Some girls who play this game don't even take their helmets off so that they can get out as quickly as possible. They also learn teamwork. Girls will have each other's gloves ready for their teammates on their way to the field and they usually have the girl with the best arm line up at the end of the line to assure a good throw home.

Relay Throw

This drill teaches the proper location for the relay throw and also helps players develop a quick turn and release of the throw.

Have the player's line up in a line stretching to the outfield about 20' apart.

The first player throws the ball to the glove side of the second player in the line. She then throws to the glove side of the player next to her.

Continue until the ball has traveled all the way down the line, and then have it brought back down the line.

Quick Hands

This drill creates a fun atmosphere, while improving hand speed and footwork.

This drill is done with a group of four or five.

One person (the thrower) begins with 2 softballs and stands about 15' from & facing the other (three or four) players in her group.

The thrower will toss a grounder or a line drive to one fielder, who will field the tossed ball and make a good, quick throw back to the tosser.

As the ball is being released by the fielder, the thrower tosses the second ball (again a grounder or line drive).

Now we have established a two-ball drill, with two balls going at the same time.

Balls can be tossed by the thrower to the same fielder in succession or maybe thrown to any of the fielders at any time.

Bat Around The Horn

This is a great drill/game for a team to build speed, accuracy in throwing, communication, and team bonding.

This game requires two teams of at least 5 players.

One team takes the field at 1st base, 2nd base, shortstop, 3rd base, and catcher. The other team is at bat. The batter hits a ground ball. This can be done from a tee, a soft toss, or by throwing the ball up and hitting it. Fly balls are strikes.

An infielder catches the ball and throws to 1st base. 1st base then throws to one of the other infielders. That fielder throws back to 1st base. 1st base then throws to the other infielder who hasn't yet touched the ball, who throws back to 1st base. The ball then goes around the horn: 1st base to short stop to 2nd base to 3rd base. Then it is thrown to the catcher.

Each fielder must touch her base before throwing except for when the ball is thrown around the horn and home. If the batter-runner can run all the way home before the ball gets home, they score a run. If the ball gets home first, they have one out. In that case, the fielders rotate one position clockwise and the next batter hits.

For every batter, each fielder has caught 3 balls and made 3 throws. Every catch and throw must be accurate or the batting team scores one run. Batters need to wear helmets. Fielders can rotate in at 3rd base if you are playing with more than 5 players on each team.

Z Drill

This drill will develop accuracy with throws and build trust with teammates.

Players form two lines facing each other about 15 – 20 feet apart. The coach flips a ball to the first player. That player throws to the player across from her.

That player immediately throws the ball to the next player in line across from her. This continues until the catcher receives the ball. The catcher then drops ball into the bucket.

After the first ball is flipped by the coach, another is tossed in by the coach.

Depending upon the skill level of the players, the coach may flip the ball immediately, or he may wait a few seconds. This continues until the coach runs out of softballs.

Wrap Around

This drill will work on all types of fielding the ball and increase endurance if continued on a regular basis.

Have two players stand 10-20 feet apart.

Player one throws a ground ball to Player Two. Player Two fields and throws back to Player One.

Player Two then runs toward Player One. She will circle Player One and return to her spot.

Player One will throw a flyball back to her.

After Player Two gets the ball, she throws it back to Player One. Then Player One throws back to Player Two.

Then Player Two gives the ground ball to Player One repeating the process.

Colored Numbers

This drill is an effective way to keep player's eyes on the ball the entire time that they are fielding.

Write numbers 1 through 5 on the balls in different colors.

Have the players field the ball and call out the color the number is written in.

When they get the hang of that, have them call out the number written.

Use permanent marker and depending on the age, determine what size to make the numbers.

Tiger

This drill is used to have everyone participate in fielding, catching and throwing.

Have everyone spread out evenly into deep infield positions. One player on first and another player for backup to the first baseman. Have an assistant be the catcher or use another player.

Start the drill by having the coach say, "ready." This is a cue for getting all the players into a ready position.

Hit grounder or fly balls to them. They will need to be sure and call it if it is a fly ball. Make sure fielders set up in proper fielding position. Once the catch is made a good throw to first base is then made. The first basemen then throws the ball to the catcher.

If a ball is missed the player missing the ball runs and retrieves the ball, runs back, and rolls the ball into the backstop while everyone else continues on with the drill. After they all have received at least one ball hit to them, tell the players to switch positions. At that time the player that is backing up the first baseman becomes the first baseman. The first baseman goes to where third would be and everyone else rotates toward first.

Mechanics Series

These are a series of drills for warm-ups and allow the players to focus on the "mechanics" of proper throwing techniques, using certain isolation drills.

1) Indian style: Have the players start approximately 10-12 yards from their partners sitting Indian style. By throwing in this position, the players isolate the upper body motion, using the glove hand for proper shoulder rotation. To help emphasize proper follow through, the players should follow through with their throwing arm elbow outside their knee, as if picking a blade of grass. This can also be done in the kneeling position with both knees on the ground, bodies square to their partners.

2) One Knee: Have the players proceed to the one knee position, stride leg in front pointing towards their partners. The players should move back to approximately 15-20 yards. This focuses on upper body mechanics and accuracy. Again, the players should follow through with their throwing elbows outside their knee with bend in the waist.

3.) Standing: Players put all three together and begin throwing from the standing position. Again, emphasize using the glove hand to point at the target as well as proper follow through (throwing wrist should brush the outside of the knee).

4) Crane: Players begin in the "crane" position. That is, with their stride leg raised in the air (knee bent), their glove hand pointing at their target, their throwing hand in the launch position (ball outside ear), players hold in this position for 2-3 seconds before releasing the ball. To ensure proper follow through, the players then take one full step towards their partner after releasing the throw. This helps the players focus on properly using their glove hand for emphasis on shoulder hip and knee rotation. For right-handed players, the left

shoulder, hip and knee point at their target and when they are done, their right shoulder hip and knee should be pointing at their target.

5) Quick throw: Players work on framing and quick release. Players catch and throw without hesitation for approximately 1-1.5 minutes straight.

6) Tags: While partners are working their "Crane" positioning, the receivers set up in the straddle position. When the throw comes in, they perform sweep tags. This allows the receivers to train as well as the throwers.

7) Throwing for distance: Once the series has gone through, continue to have the players back up until they are able to make accurate, strong throws DIRECTLY to the receiver. No lob throws. This allows arm strengthening.

Ready for Anything

This drill will effectively prepare a player to be ready for any kind of hit that could come their way.

Have one person to throw the ball and one to receive.

Have the players form a line about 30 to 40 feet away from the person that is throwing the ball.

Tell the players to charge the ball. Also tell them that they could expect almost anything: grounder, pop fly, or a line drive right to them – anything.

Continue drill and switch sides.

Grounder Flyball Game

This drill is a good for speed, fielding and personal effort.

Line all of the players up at third base. Hit a hard grounder to the first person in line. As soon as they field throw it back to the coach.

The coach will then immediately throw a high fly ball to first making the player hustle to get it.

The player catches it and throws it back to the coach.

The coach then hits a ground ball to third, thus making them run back across to get it, return the ball, and proceed to the end of the line.

Speed up the drill as players advance.

Ram

This drill is competitive, quick and an effective way to keep players motivated in the game to hustle and get a little dirty.

Set up 2 players between 1st and 2nd and the other between 2nd and 3rd

Place cones just behind the baseline about 15'-20' apart

The coach will try to hit the balls past the two infielders

Bobbles are OK as long as the ball doesn't pass the cones. When the fielder misses the ball then the next player is up.

Keep a record and the best score wins.

Over the Head

This drill is an effective way to initiate a game like situation in how to react to a fly ball that could be going over the players head.

Line up the players next to the coach or individual throwing the balls.

Have the first player step out about 15'-20' in front and facing the thrower.

The thrower will throw/hit a fly ball that goes over the player's head, either to the right or the left side of the player.

The player must then tuck her glove and run in the direction the ball is traveling

The player should make the catch under the ball and return the ball to the thrower.

Repeat with all players in line

Have the players stand closer for added difficulty upon advancement.

Outfield Fly

This is a great drill to exercise communication and proper outfield functions in game like situations.

Place half the team in left field and the rest in center. The coaches hit a flyball in between the first two outfielders in each line.

They both go for the ball with one catching it and the other properly backing up the fielder.

If the ball happens to get by both fielders then they will use a relay throw to get the ball back to the coach.

Make sure that girls communicate with each other as to who will catch the ball.

Knockout

This drill is an effective way to bring some fun competition to the team while still exercising the fundamentals of the game.

The players are divided into two teams. One team at third base and one team at second base.

Each coach stands on the opposite end at home and first base and hit/throws grounders or fly balls to their team across the field.

Each coach has a catcher who feeds the ball to the coach and also must catch all balls if possible.

To complete the play the player must catch the ball successfully and make a catchable throw to their catcher for a point.

This goes on for about 3 minutes with the winner watching the others run or getting a treat.

This can also be played indoors on a gym floor.

Crossfire

This drill is an effective way to practice good communication skills as well as keeping the players focused and alert while fielding, running, hitting. and catching.

Use 2 hitters and catchers, and two or more fielders.

Place one set of catcher and hitter half way between 1st base and Home, the other set between 3rd and Home

Place one fielder at shortstop and another at second base. Have the other girls flank the fielders about 10 feet back.

The hitter between 1st base and home will hit to short stop and the hitter between 3rd and home will hit to 2nd base. The balls should "crossover" one another essentially.

Once the fielder has fielded and thrown the ball back to the catcher, the fielder will rotate clockwise and the next player will take her position.

Have the hitters hit about 15 times, then rotate with the catchers. When they have both hit 15 each, the hitters and catchers will rotate to the field and 4 fielders will come in to hit and catch.

Clockwork

This drill contains variations of throwing, fielding, conditioning, and communication.

Set up a cutoff approximately 50 ft. from the catcher and 5 or 6 outfielders each spread out from right to left, approximately 50 ft. from cutoff.

Start by hitting a ball to the girl farthest left. She throws to cutoff. Cutoff throws home. After throwing to cutoff, the fielder then runs to take her spot. After throwing home, the girl at cutoff runs home to become catcher, and the catcher is to run to the open spot in the outfield.

Four Corners

This drill is an effective way to incorporate a quick warm-up, work on fielding ground balls, throwing accuracy, and pivoting to make the next throw.

Players are located at 3rd base fielding position, 2nd base (on bag), 1st base (on bag) and at catcher. All other players are lined up at 3rd base coaching box.

The coach hits ground ball to 3rd base, who throws to 2nd base, who throws to 1st base, who throws to catcher.

After they throw, the player then sprints to the position she threw to.

The next player in line then assumes 3rd base and the drill starts over.

When everyone has been through, place the players at 1st base and the drill goes from 1st base to 2nd base to 3rd base to catcher.

This drill provides a quick warm-up and works on fielding ground balls, throwing accuracy, and pivoting to make the next throw.

Stuffed Animal

This drill is variation of other throwing accuracy drills, but with more of a target if there are not enough people around to hit and catch for you.

Get a stuffed animal and put it on a chair by 1st base. If you have a net, put the nest behind the chair to stop the ball. If not, put the chair near home. Have a coach hit ground balls to shortstop.

The player fields the ball and makes a throw trying to knock the stuffed animal off the chair.

The ball must be fielded properly or the player receives no points. Have a time limit (about 5 minutes) and keep track of how many hits the toy gets.

Triangle

This drill is an easy way to keep the players alert while practicing.

Divide the team up into 3 groups.

The first group stands between first base and second base.

The second group stands at short stop.

The third group stands at home plate with a coach and the catcher standing a little to the side of the plate.

The coach hits the ball to the first group, and the first girl in line for the first group catches it and throws it to the girl in the second group, while running to the second group position.

The second group girl that catches the ball throws it to home plate while running there.

Continue until all the players have been through all the positions.

Hit the Bucket

This drill improves throwing accuracy and footwork in the infield.

Divide the team into two groups. Half are positioned at short stop and the other half are positioned at second base.

Mark off a starting point that the girls must stay behind until a ground ball is hit to them by a coach at home plate. Each group alternates players fielding ground balls and throwing to home plate where two stacked buckets are located.

Each time a player hits the top bucket on a bounce 1 point is awarded. Hitting the bucket without a bounce gets 2 points. The first group to 10 points is the winner.

Star Game

This drill is a sufficient way to have infielder's learning to get rid of the ball quickly.

Infielders stand at their positions (except the pitcher)and the ball starts at the catcher, who throws to the second baseman.

The second baseman then throws to the third baseman.

The third baseman then throws to the first baseman.

The first baseman then throws to the shortstop.

The short stop finishes with throwing back to the catcher.

While this is happening, a runner is running the bases. They leave at the same time as the catcher starts the cycle.

The fielders usually start to move towards the middle, making it easier on them. Let them do that for a while, until it gets too easy, then make them start backing up. After they get a few steps in the grass the faster runners start making it close. (the runners like to see a dropped or missed ball)

8 Ball

This drill is progressive way to warm-up before a game, or just before practice.

Player stands with feet shoulder width apart, puts throwing arm up at 90 degree angle, holds elbow with glove, and throws ball to partner just using wrist action. Player sits with legs spread and has arm in same position only this time she can use from her elbow up and throws the ball to her partner.

Player remains sitting, only now she can rotate her hips and turn her upper torso to throw the ball. Follow through is not necessary yet. There is an emphasis on using the glove arm or elbow to direct throw.

Player now goes to one knee. She rotates her hips and upper torso and throws the ball, only now she puts the emphasis on following through across her knee which is raised.

Player now stands with glove arm closest to partner, and feet shoulder width apart. Using all of the above steps, she throws the ball concentrating on follow through, only she cannot move her feet.

Player now goes to the post position as in pitching, and throws the ball using the above steps. Emphasis in this step is balance at the post position.

Player now uses all the steps above and crow hops and throws the ball to his/her partner. Emphasis in this step is proper technique of the crow hop.

Finally, the last step is long toss.

3 – 2 Run Game

This drill provides game-like situational pressure to make accurate throws during plays.

Separate the players into two teams. (One will be fielding and one will be batting)

Place 3 balls on the ground evenly spaced, about 3/4 of the way from third base to home.

The fielding team has a third baseman and a group at second base.

The other team is at bat (without bats). When the coach yells, "Go", the batter (runner) runs as fast as he/she can to first base and on to second.

The fielder at third base runs to the first ball and makes a throw to a teammate at second base, then goes to the second ball and makes a throw to the same fielder at second base and does the same thing with the third ball.

If the runner gets to second base first, or if the fielder makes a bad throw or bad catch, the batters get 1 point (you can use any value you want). If the fielders get all 3 balls to second base before the runner gets there, no points are awarded.

After every player on the fielding team has had a chance to make the plays at second base then the teams will switch.

Glove off

This drill emphasizes hand-eye coordination when throwing, catching and fielding the ball.

The drill uses a whiffle ball and a plastic bat.

First set the bases at about 40 feet apart and divide your team in two.

One team fields and the other bats. Fielders do not use their gloves. (This teaches that the hands are the real tools in catching the ball)

The ball is pitched from about 20 feet away. The batter has only three chances to hit the ball. (There are no balls or walks in this drill.)

Once the ball is hit, the batter must run the bases until she reaches home plate or is tagged out. The fielders must always try to tag the runner out at first.

You bat the entire line up and then you change sides. We usually do this drill twice a week for about 20 minutes at a very fast pace.

1, 2, 3 Drill

This is a line drive and pop up fielding drill which teaches players to catch three types of fly balls. (Line drive right at them, line drive that they must stretch for, and last a flyball that they must sprint to catch)

Line your players up in a single file line, players should start on the fair line just behind first base at the edge of the outfield grass.

The coach will be in right-center field with a bucket of balls.

The players will be running in a straight line about 50 to 60 feet away from the coach. (Running from first towards second.) One player at a time with their gloves.

The coach starts by throwing a line drive right at the players and the player catches it and while still running

The coach throws the second ball in front of the same player making her reach to catch it, while the player is still running

The coach throws the third ball, which is a high pop fly out away from the player that she must track down and catch it.

After player one has taken her turn she retreats and picks up the three balls and returns to the back of the line and it is time for the next player.

Keys To This Drill

Once the player starts running (she never stops nor hesitates) she sprints all the way, catching all the balls on the run.

Once the players catches a ball she quickly throws it down and looks for the next ball.

There is a big difference between running and sprinting. We like our players to sprint while doing this drill.

Gary LeLand

Hitting Drills

Power Hitting

This drill is a great way maximize power in a batters swing

This drill requires a punching bag (about $45 dollars at any sporting goods store) and somewhere to hang it.

Batters will take their stance with the punching bag slightly in line with the batters front foot.

The batter will swing, make contact with the bag, and then proceed to follow through with their extension pushing the bag.

The batter can adjust where she stands and makes contact with the bag depending on what pitch she would like to work on.

Blind Tee Drill

This is a fun drill to increase a batters concentration and test their muscle memory.

Set up a tee

The batter will hit 5 balls and then put on a blindfold to attempt to hit 5 more balls.

Remove the blind fold and move to position the tee in the location to where another pitch would be

The batter will hit 5 balls and then put the blindfold on again and attempt to hit 5 more balls.

You can split the players into 2 teams and the players that get the most hits when blindfolded will win

This is great for loosening up players before big games and great for team bonding.

Weight Hittings

This drill is an effective way to create proper muscle memory and gain strength in your bottom hand when hitting.

The batter will use a 5-10 pound dumbbell (depending on the batters strength) and position your hands on the dumbbell as if you are it was the bat.

Leading with your elbow the dumbbell should follow a straight line from your back shoulder to the front side of your chest.

This motions should be slow and cause resistance in your bottom hand.

Do 5 sets of 10 reps with small breaks in between.

Downward Resistance

This drill is an effective way to break players of the habit of dropping the barrel of the bat and popping up the ball when they hit.

One player at a time will take her at-bat stance.

The coach will stand where the umpire would normally stand and hold the top of the barrel on the bat.

The player will be instructed to take her swing as the coach is still holding the barrel of the bat up.

As the coach is holding up the barrel of the bat the player is feeling that resistance and is making the correct motions to pull the bat away from the coach's hands.

The coach will then release the bat and the player will finish her swing.

The player will not hit the coach when she finishes her swing.

If the coach still feels uncomfortable with this then just take a step back when releasing the bat.

Contact on Commands

This is a great drill for players to work on reaction time with taking a particular bat swing for different pitches.

Line up 3-5 batters about 4-5 feet apart with their bats

The coach will call out a certain pitch (high outside, low inside, drop ball, curve, and screw) and the batters will take the appropriate swing and freeze where they would make contact with the ball.

The coach will observe and if wrong the player drops for 5 pushups and is out. The correct players remain in the game and sets for another pitch command.

Motion Hittings

This drill is a great way to ensure that batters become aware of the importance in using the lower body to increase power in their swing.

The batter will step up to bat with their front foot on the back line of the batter's box

The batter will take a step with their back foot and then with their front foot to end close to their usual stance in the batter's box.

As the batter takes her last step the coach will soft toss the ball.

The batter sets her hands quickly and takes her swing.

This should not be a slapping motion. The batter just has to be quick enough with her footwork and setting her hands to hit the ball at her usual stance.

Tee Opposite Field Hittings

This drill is an effective way to perfect hitting to the opposite field.

Set up a tee at home plate. Also set up 4 cones designating the zones of a left handed hitter and a right handed hitter that would hit to the opposite field.

Take 10 softballs and locate where the laces are closest together and have that part facing you. Then mark an "X" on one of the laces.

The balls will be placed on the tee, with the "X" facing the backstop and the laces are vertical to the ground.

For left handed hitters the "X" will be on the right and for right handed hitters the "X" will be on the right.

These will give hitters a target to aim for in practicing hitting to the opposite field.

Hit 10 balls and then rotate hitters.

Adjust swing and continue drill until all balls that are hit are directed to the opposite field.

Fungo Competitions

This is a fun drill to help with players keeping their eye on the ball when hitting.

Divide the players into 2 even teams with one lined up on the first base line and the other on the third baseline.

Player will step up and 5 ball for each team will be lined up about 2 feet apart and about 4 feet away from the back stop.

The players will take their stance at the ball on the end and on the coaches command will squat and pick up the ball, soft toss it to themselves, hit it into the fence, and continue with the remaining 4 balls.

The first player to hit all 5 of the balls into the fence first wins a point for their team.

Hitting Conditionings

This drill will work all muscles involved in hitting to build maximum endurance and power in a player's swing.

Set up 5 different hitting stations along the fence behind home plate and one tee at home plate.

The hitting stations will be soft toss with basketballs, whiffle balls, front hand hitting, back hand hitting, and regular soft toss with softballs.

Split the players into two equal teams. One team will be feeding and shagging the balls and the other will be going through the stations.

The first hitter will begin with the station closes to third base. When finished with that station the next player will follow.

The hitters will go through all 5 stations and then step up to the plate to hit 1 ball of the tee, run to retrieve the ball and return it back to the bucket of balls at home plate. (Make sure to yell "BALL" before hitting to warn others that may not be paying attention)

After, return back to the stations and repeat the process.

This can be completed by time or by how many times a player can complete the stations. But the drill is to be done at a very quick pace.

Core Strength

This drill is an effective way to gain core muscles for more power when hitting

Each hitter will drop down on her right knee (similar to a lunge position)

With a 5 or 10 pound weight the players will begin holding the weight on their right side by their right knee. The players will use their core to lift the weight over their knee to the other side. And repeat completing 3 sets of 10

After the third set switch knees and repeat on the other side.

Hit and Run

This drill is an effective way to maintain focus and stamina no matter what condition a player may be in when up to bat.

This drill is set up in a soft toss situation with a net with a group of 3 batters.

The Coach will quickly feed the batter 20 balls and then the batter will take off for 2 laps around the field.

The Coach will begin with the next batter.

The batters should make it back to hit again with a small amount of time to rest and hit another 20 balls and run another 2 laps.

The batters should complete 6 laps and then switch out the groups.

Pressure Scrimmage

This drill will aid in gaining confidence for players in pressure situations up at the plate.

This drill is set up as a scrimmage.

Each player that goes up to bat will begin with a 2-2 count and have 1 out for their team.

This game is fast paced keeping the players moving.

Points are gained based on how many bases are earned.

Points are also earned for each foul ball hit, but only if the batter makes contact and is safe at the base.

Bat Colors

This drill is an effective way to encourage players to keep their eyes on the ball as they reach contact point with the bat.

Take a players bat and use 3 different colors of electric tape on the three zones of the bat (End, sweet spot, and lower half)

As the ball is soft tossed the batter will swing the bat and call out the color of where the ball was hit on the bat.

Two Tee Target Drill

This drill is an effective way to practice contact point and ball placement.

Have your swing warmed up for hitting and set up one tee directly on the plate and another in line with it two feet in front of the plate.

Set the heights either the same or have the one in front slightly lower than the tee on home plate.

Assume the ready position and upon the hitting command attempt to hit the ball on the back tee to make contact with the ball on the front tee.

You may adjust tees to work on inside and outside pitches as well.

Surprise Soft Toss

This drill is an effective way to improve reaction time while keeping balance and power when hitting.

This drill is set up in a soft toss situation.

The soft tosser will toss the ball into the air (a little higher than usual) and then say "ball"

The batter will open his/her eyes and make the decision whether or not to swing.

If the batter swings then the focus is to stay balanced and make solid contact while keeping quick hands and hitting fundamentals.

Pressure Execution Plus

This drill is an effective way to execute offensive fundamentals under pressure.

Line up the team in batting order at home plate with bats warmed up for the drill.

Make a team goal of hitting the entire line-up with only one or two errors allowed. If goal is not met then the team will have a conditioning exercise of the coach's choice for that round.

The coach will give the command from third base (ex. Base hit, squeeze, sac, hit & run, opposite field, etc.) and then, from live pitching or a machine, the ball will be pitched and begin the count of correct execution or error.

3 Plate Drill

This drill will help with simulating live situational hitting without having to use a pitcher.

Set up three home plates staggered and have a machine or front tosser ready.

After each pitch make adjustments to one of the other two home plates for another pitch to become more comfortable with adjusting to certain pitches like in a game situation.

V Drill

This drill is used to develop lead arm extension and the sensation of unloading the wrist properly to deliver the bat head through the zone with a snap and not a drag.

Set up using a tee or soft toss and having a mini bat is preferred.

The batter will set up his/her hitting stance using only the lead arm (with the mini bat or chocking up on a regular bat) positioning the barrel of the bat next to his/her back shoulder.

When making the swing, lead with the knob of the bat towards the ball (making a "V" with your wrist and the bat) then release the barrel to drive through the ball, letting the wrist roll only AFTER impact with the ball.

The W Drill

The "W" drill conditions pitchers in fielding the bunt, making a firm throw, and developing mental toughness.

Draw a large "W" in the dirt.

Stand on the pitching rubber with the "W" facing the pitcher.

The first pitcher throws a pitch to the catcher, drives off the mound to her right, fields a rolled ground ball or bunt from the batter's box, makes a firm throw to first base, and returns to the pitching rubber.

The pitcher then throws her second pitch, drives downhill and fields a rolled ball at the top of the "W", makes a firm throw to second base, then back pedals full speed to the pitching rubber.

The pitcher then throws her third pitch, drives downhill, fields a rolled ball to her left, makes a firm throw to third base, then back pedals full speed to the pitching rubber.

The second pitcher then toes the rubber and starts her round of the same drill, and then the third pitcher, etc.

This drill is to be full speed throughout.

Target Practice

This drill is an effective way to work on ball placement and contact point when hitting the ball deeper in the strike zone.

Set up a tee in the desired location that the batter feels the need to improve on

Set up cones in the field to designate zones that the ball should be hit to depending on the pitch.

Then have the batter hit the ball aiming for the specified area and adjust swing accordingly

When the player becomes more advanced set up tees 20 to 40 feet in a specific direction and aim to knock the ball off. Adjust distance according to increased improvement.

Tennis Can Lidss

This drill is a simple way to encourage snap in your swing and better visual tracking of the ball.

Collect tennis can lids

Set up in a front toss situation and throw the lids Frisbee style towards the batter. Alternate which edge is up to imitate curve, screwball, etc.

Tees

This drill is a great way for players that are having trouble rotating their hips to gain more movement.

Place a ball on a tee at about hip height.

Have the batter position her bat behind her lower back and take a normal batting stance and then pivot her hips and knock the ball off the tee with the bat.

Then place the tee at the desired impact point (for inside and outside pitches) and have the batter continue to pivot and knock off the ball, but in the different ball positions for technique in hitting these pitches.

Bunting Game

This drill is an effective way to improve bunting skills, ball placement, and also have a good time with the entire team.

Draw sections in the dirt in front of home plate with numbers representing point value based on what the coach considers the perfect bunt.

Divide the batters into teams and set up either live pitching or a machine. (Machines tend to have bouncier balls so make sure to make the point sections bigger if you use a machine and then explain to the batters why.)

Each batter takes a turn bunting and is awarded the point value of the section that the ball stops in (Not lands in). After every player has taken a turn, total up the points and reward the winners.

After, allow the batters to take turns in drawing their own sections and assigning point values. No matter where the values are placed the batters will still be learning to place their bunts.

Barriers

This drill will provide feedback to whether a batter is unlocking her elbows before her shoulders and getting too wide in the swing.

Have the batter take a stance one bat length away from a net, wall, or fence. (Preferably a net to avoid damage to the bat) The batter will then take a swing and acquire immediate feedback of an arm extension error if the barrier is hit.

Adjust swing and continue drill for improvement.

Knee Hitting

This drill allows concentration on the upper half of the body during a swing

Set up a net as if you were about to do a tee drill but instead set a medium sized orange cone where the tee would typically be.

Have the batter take a stance kneeling on their back knee and their front leg should be straight out in front towards the net.

Place the ball on the cone and have them hit. This will allow them to concentrate on proper hand and arm movement without worrying about the legs.

The coach should be the one observing while another player resets the ball on the cone. This allows the coach to provide feedback to aid the batter and also gets other players involved as well.

Soft- Toss

This drill is a well-known drill to get more bat power and work on any part of the swing that a player may need to work on.

Set up in a soft toss situation. The tosser should set themselves at the batting side of the batter and ahead of the batter as well.

Each toss should be approximately tossed at the hip of the batter. The toss should be crisp, but not too fast and out in front of the batter. Practice the toss to get it correct.

Now, toss the balls to the batter's desire and focus on proper hitting mechanics

Miss/Miss/Hit

This drill is a great way to improve bat control, contact point, and keeping your eye on the ball.

Set up with soft-toss, machine, or live pitching.

Use a series of three pitches to teach players to watch the ball. With the first pitch, the batter swings over the ball. The second pitch, the batter swings under. The third pitch, the batter hits the ball.

Repeat this drill until they can do it every time and then switch up the pitches. (pitch one, hit the top of the ball. Second, the bottom of the ball. Etc.)

Different Objects

This drill will improve concentration on the ball for a batter.

Set up in a soft-toss situation.

Instead of using only softballs use golf wiffle balls, ping-pong balls, pinto beans, or anything that has players concentrating on a smaller than usual target or on a target that moves randomly, rather than moving in a straight line.

Balls and Strikes

This drill is an effective way for batters to become accustomed to what may be called balls and strikes.

Have a live pitching situation set up.

Have the batter take her stance and then have the pitcher pitch the ball.

The batter will only watch the ball all the way into the glove and then call the pitch a ball or a strike. (It is amazing what a batter thinks is a ball)

Then when the calls are becoming more accurate or correct, start naming the pitches.

The Hawk Eye

This drill will improve a player's ability to keep her eye on the ball.

During pitching exercises have a batter step in like in a live game situation.

With each pitch the batter will not swing, but instead read the balls rotation, name of the pitch, and provide the feedback to the coach and pitcher. (Have the coach confirm if correct or incorrect).

The Bat Thing

This drill is a great way to learn to rotate hips and adjust height with the bending at the knees for higher or lower pitches.

You will have one pitcher, one batter, and one fielder.

The hitter will take her stance with the bat behind her lower back.

Have the pitcher pitch the ball slow and flat as the batter will have to use her hips and adjust her height with her legs to make contact with the ball.

This works for both indoors and outdoors.

Batting Beam

This drill will aid in a player's balance throughout her swing.

Create a batting beam with a piece of 2" X 4" approximately 4' long and nail two cross pieces, about 18" long to each end of the main piece.

Set up a soft- toss situation and have the batter stand on the beam.

When the batter takes a swing the batter should remain on the beam throughout the swing.

Continue drill and make adjustments, such as standing more on the balls of your feet, for better balance.

Hands to the Ball

This drill is an effective way to practice bringing hands to the ball.

Set up with a batter and a soft- tosser directly 3 ft in front of the batter.

The batter will take her stance, but with the bat resting on her back shoulder.

The ball will then be tossed and the batter will attempt to hit the ball with the knob of the bat (end cap on the handle). NO SWINGING ALLOWED.

Upon improvement adjust tosses to different locations (high, low, inside, outside).

Pepper Game

This drill is a great way to develop bat control and short, quick swings.

Have a batter set up approximately 22 feet away from three fielders who will position themselves two feet apart.

The ball will begin with one of the fielders who will then toss the ball to be hit back using a short, quick, downward stroke. This should be a quick ground ball back to the fielder depending on the placement of the toss. (Inside pitch to the fielder to your left) Then repeat.

To make the drill more difficult use two balls at once keeping the hitter consistently ready.

Dizzy Lizzy

This is a great drill to loosen up your players while getting a little batting practice in the process.

Make two teams. One team in the infield (On first and third base) and one team lined up to bat.

All the hits will be made from a tee. Before making the swing the batter will put the knob of the bat to her forehead and the other end on the ground. Then the batter will spin around 5-7 times and take her swing and runs the bases.

Where ever the ball is hit, the two infield players must run to where the ball ended up before the batter makes it back to home plate.

This will loosen up any uptight players in a hurry!

Drop

This drill will increase bat speed and reaction time.

Utilize some type of back-stop and a bucket or old milk crate with one player standing on the milk crate.

The player standing on the milk crate will hold the ball at the shoulder height and drop it straight into the strike zone.

The batter must see the ball and react fast enough to hit it.

Drop the balls as quickly or slowly as desired.

Basketball

This drill will aid in improving follow-through with your swing.

First, get some old basketballs and take most of the air out of them.

Proceed to take a full swing from a side toss pitch or off of a construction cone and make sure to follow all the way through.

Make sure to use regular sized bats during this drill.

Gary LeLand

Running Drills

Stations

This drill is for building leg strength, improving explosion off the bag when running, and speed.

Coaches will set up the field with ladders going from home to first, small hurdles or cones, 2 feet apart, from first to second, and softballs spread about 2-3 feet apart between second and third.

The first player will use quick feet to put each foot inside each the ladder rung all the way to first base. Then the next player will start.

From first to second the players will hop over the cones or hurdles bringing their knees all the way up to their chest.

From second to third the players will lunge pick up the softball to either the right or left of the player, pick it up, and move it over to the other side, set it down, lunge, and repeat. The next player will to the same, but the ball may be on a different side.

Then from third base the player will jog back to home plate to begin again.

Softball Snake

This is a fun drill to bond a team and get some running into a workout.

All of the girls will begin at home plate and run along the fence line one behind the other

The person in the front will hold a softball and everyone will begin running

While running the person in the front will toss the ball up so that the player behind her can catch it and to the same until the ball reaches the last player.

When the last player receives the ball that player runs a little bit faster to get to the front of the line and begin the process again.

Give the players a goal of running the entire field and having all of the girls being the leader at least once and without dropping the ball.

When the players no longer find this to be a challenge then have all of then become the leader twice before making it back to home plate! Keep if FUN!

Speed Conditioning

This drill is great for the off-season in increasing a player's speed

All players will begin at home plate.

One player at a time will take her batting stance, take a swing, and take off through first base.

When the entire team has completes this the players will line up to run a double and then back to the end of the line, run a triple, then finally the players will run all the bases.

Now, the first runner, again, will take a swing and take the turn at first and then wait at first for the second player to swing and then she takes off to second. She will take the turn at second and then wait on second for the third player to take her swing before going to third.. And repeat with all players.

Once all players have finished that part they will begin again.

The goal is to incorporate sorter and longer sprinting distances with small breaks in between for maximum result in speed.

This will exhaust the players and should be done with 3-4 days of break before repeating the drill again.

Tag Up Drill

This drill will help base runners that get caught taking off on fly balls without tagging up on the base.

Have runners at each base, players in each position, and then have the coach hit from home plate (hitting mostly fly balls and some low flys, and popups close to the infield)

This will simulate game situations and to make sure that the runners are paying attention to where the ball is going before just immediately taking off on bat contact.

Turn, Dive, Run, Slide

This drill is a fun way to practice all basic base running fundamentals.

All players will begin at home plate. The players will take a swing and then take off to first as if to run to second, but only take a 3 step lead off and then dive back to the base.

The runner will quickly stand up and run to second, pop-up slide into the bag, take a 3 step lead off, and dive back to second base.

The runner will quickly recover again and take off to third, hook slide to the right of the bag to avoid a tag, recover, take a 3 step lead off, and dive back to the base.

Then the runner will recover and take off into a sprint through home plate and back to the end of the line.

There should not be any break time for runners during this drill.

After the runner in front takes off to second base then the next runner may begin.

Crowns

This drill is great for building a players strength and endurance when running. This is a great off season drill.

Line up all of the players in partners at home plate. (Partners will encourage each other)

The first group will jog out to the foul pole in right field and drop and do 10 push-ups correctly.

The second group will follow when the first group finishes their push-up and so on..

The first group now jogs backwards to the second base fielding position, drops and completes 15 correct sit-ups (Might want to set up a cone halfway between 1st and 2nd to mark this spot)

Then that group lunges out to the fence in center field and completes 15 jumping jacks

They then jog to the short stop position and complete 20 crunches

Then proceed to the left field foul pole and complete 10 more push-ups correctly

Finally the group will build up to a sprint back to home plate.

Continue this drill about 5 times and then add a time limit to push the players!

Pre Run

This drill will warm players up before games to prevent pulled muscles and build endurance.

Players will begin with a slow jog from the foul line to center field and back.

Now the players conduct one of the everyday stretches (Making sure to keep them even i.e. If you stretch the right leg then you must stretch the left leg as well)

Then the girls will lunge out until they reach 2nd base and then back to the foul line.

The girls will then again conduct another stretch.

Now the girls will do but kicks till they reach the second base line and then back.

Another stretch.

Frankenstein walk (Holding arms straight out and kicking the palms of your hands) to the 2nd base line and back.

Another stretch.

Then the girls will finish with buildup running. Jog slowly and build up to 50% speed, then 75% speed, then 100% speed. Continuing the stretching in between.

Partner Running

This drill will promote teamwork as well as endurance, and improved hand-eye coordination.

Have the girl's partner up and line up at home plate with one softball per group.

The first group will face each other shuffling in a fielding position while rolling the ball to their partner (slightly ahead of their partner) as they travel down the first base line all the way to the foul pole. The second group will begin when the first group reaches first base.

After reaching the foul pole then that group will jog side-by-side along the fence, tossing the ball in the air to each other, all the way to the other foul pole.

After reaching the foul pole in left field then have the partners walk, one in front of the other, back to home plate while tossing the ball up to each other. The player in the back tosses it about 3ft above and in front of the player in front, while walking. Player in front then gently tosses it up and the player in the back catches it until the the partners make it back to home plate.

After the entire team makes it around once, challenge the groups to speed up and when the ball is dropped or another group passes them then the group sits where they are and that group is out.

Winning group sits out of 10 push-ups, running, or sit-ups.

One Ball, Two Ball

This drill will build endurance of players as well as work on the accuracy of the throws made.

Evenly spread out the players at each base.

The ball will begin at home plate and will throw the ball to first.

The person at fist will throw to second. This is continued all the way around the bases with each player running to where they threw the ball and waiting at the end of the line for another turn.

When players are used to this, throw in a second ball.

When players are used to this, yell out "reverse" and reverse the direction in which the ball was being thrown.

Each time the ball is dropped or a bad throw is made the players must drop their gloves and run around the bases until they reach their spot and begin again.

Have a goal of 10 or 15 times the ball goes around the bases without making a bad throw or missing the ball.

Agility Base Running

This drill is great for conditioning, building endurance, and base running.

All runners will begin at home plate

The first runner will step in the box, take a swing and take off to first base taking the turn at first.

The runner will then shuffle, keeping her butt down like taking a fielding stance, until she reaches second.

After tagging second she will jog backwards and 3/4 of the way to third turn around and sprint to tag third, continue running, and slide into home.

The runner will then go to the end of the line and continue the drill.

After the runner reaches first base the next player should begin.

This is a continuous and fast paced drill.

Base Coaching

This drill can be fun for players to learn to always watch the first base coach, react to the signals, and execute with proper footwork.

Runners will be lined up at home plate

The runners will take a swing and proceed to run to first.

Within the first 4 to 5 steps the runner should look at the first base coach and depending on the signals the coach has designated the runner will either take the turn, or run through the base.

When runners become more advanced add the third base coach.

When runners are signaled to take the turn at first the third base coach will give another signal.

At the end of each sequence the runners will proceed to the back of the line at home plate and continue.

Pitch Anticipating

This drill will provide base runners with more experience and practice in reading the trajectory of the pitch and eliminate hesitation in a game.

Have a few runners at each base, with a pitcher and catcher in position.

The pitcher will make a pitch and the runners will take their lead and then make the decision to whether the pitch is in the dirt or is a passed ball and steal or stay.

The coach will be standing by watching and if a runner hesitates on their decision then he/she will have to run out to the outfield, touch the fence and then proceed to the next base.

Each pitch the runner will go to the end of the line at the next base so that the players are constantly rotating.

When runners become more confident and are predicting the pitch more accurately have the coach, on passed balls and pitches in the dirt, yell different ways to slide into the next base (head first, hook slide, pop-up).

4, 3, 2, 1

This drill is for both fundamental base running and conditioning! This makes for running with a purpose! It's continuous, so it's tough!

The entire team starts at home plate and one at a time, each athlete swings like she is really hitting from the box, then sprints down through first base, touching the front of the bag and continuing to run through the bag.

They then jog back to home plate to the end of the line and complete this four times.

They then swing like they are really hitting and sprint all the way to second base, touching the inside corner of both first and second base.

They then jog around until back to home plate in line again, a total of three times.

Then swinging once again like they are really hitting, then sprinting all the way to third base, touching the inside corner at all three bases.

Then jogging back to home plate in line again. Two times!

Then finishing with a swing like they have really just hit the ball and sprinting around all bases for a home run, touching all inside corners one time.

Think, Run and React

This drill is great for working on the basic fundamentals of base running.

Players line up at home plate

The first player swing an imaginary bat and sprint to first base running through through the base and two steps past, then look to the right for an overthrow.

After all the players take the run to first base then the players line up in foul territory by first base.

First player takes a two-step lead, looking at home for imaginary pitch. The coach in player's line-of-sight and holds up any number of fingers on one hand, simulating the ball hit by a batter. The player yells out the number and sprints to second base, loops out before second, lines up and sprints to third.

(Optional: slide into second base)

After that sequence the players line up in foul territory next to third. One at a time, they take the lead and upon command from the coach, come back, check the catch of an imaginary fly ball in the outfield, tag up and score.

Players line up at home plate while the coach is beyond first base in the baseline to second. Each player swings and 'hits' a double sprints and loops out before first and runs to second, while avoiding running out of running path and into the coach.

Players take their lead off at second looking at home plate. The coach is in their line-of-sight and holds up two hands. Players yell out the correct number of fingers the coach is holding up and sprint to third, loop out and run through third, staying 'off the grass' and score.

(Other options: a. Hit a triple. Follow with a lead from third and score on a passed ball. b. Hit a home run. c. Hit a single to the outfield, round first, and coach yells 'go' or 'back'. If coach yells 'go', players have the option of sliding into second.)

Team Sliding

This drill provides fun competition while learning and gaining confidence with sliding

Divide the team into groups of four.

Each group of four should spread out and form a square (about twenty by twenty feet) marked on the field, with a "base" in each corner and a player on each base.

At the whistle, the player at home takes off for first, sliding in. When she touches the bag, the player standing there at first takes off for second.

When she slides in, the runner on second base takes off toward third.

This continues around the horn until the player who began at home gets back home again. Whichever team does this the fastest is the winner.

If you do not have enough room to have all your groups going at once, then you can use a stopwatch to see which group is the fastest.

Tennis Ball

This drill is productive for players to work on leading off and speed.

The runner is on 1st base in her ready position (ready for her lead off).

Another player or coach is a short distance from her, in the base path from 1st to 2nd base.

The coach holds a tennis ball at eye height. As the ball is dropped on a piece of flat wood, the runner leaves the base and attempts to catch the ball before it bounces off the wood a second time.

The distance for this drill is determined by the skill level of the runners, but start out close so that she can easily catch the ball and slowly move back to challenge her.

Team Exercises

This drill is great for the beginning of practice or as a warm-up, incorporate these running exercises.

Players run straight ahead at 3/4 speed. They should concentrate arm swing and run at 3/4 speed, accelerate to full speed, and then slow down (about 30 yds.)

Players move sideways by sliding their right foot out and following with their left foot. They should avoid crossing or hitting their feet together. Players should keep their shoulders level and facing home plate.

Players lead off from the base. They should be standing with feet parallel to the base next to them. Have them swing their left leg over towards their right to start a run towards another base. Run to the other base. Make sure they do no turn or swivel their feet and run to the next base.

Players keep their left foot on base. Their right foot should be behind the base facing the next base. Run to the next base.

Runners should shuffle 3 to 4 times and then return to an imaginary base. Put their left foot on the base and look towards the outfield. They will then run on your command of "go".

Scrambled Eggs

This drill is a fun and challenging way to teach players to keep their hands over their head to have a nice clean slide

Line the players up at 1st base. Use 2 raw eggs. Tell them to hold on to the eggs, run towards second, slide, and don't break the eggs.

Don't give each girl two eggs – use the same two eggs over and over.

After they've each made the trip to 2nd base twice, put a rope across the path — about three feet in front of 2nd base for them to slide under. (This will give them the incentive to stay low on the slide. Make sure the rope is held very loosely!)

After they've done that two times, take the eggs and have one of the players come and look at them. Point out the fact that there are lots of little cracks in the eggs and that they're getting pretty weak.

Get the girls to slide into 2nd, pop-up and run to 3rd and slide. Then they should run to 1st and hand the eggs off.

Running Game

This drill provides intense competition and a great base running and conditioning exercise.

Split the team evenly into two separate groups.

One group will line up at second base and the other at home.

On the signal, one player from each team runs the bases until she reaches the base she started out at and tags the next runner in line and she runs the bases.

This is done until all the runners have run. Whoever reaches their base first, wins.

Thunder Game

This drill is a effective exercise to promote speed, agility, and some in-fielding work.

This game is played with 2 teams. One team is at bat with a tee or soft-toss, the other team has one fielder on third base and one on first base.

The batter hits the ball off the tee or from a soft-toss as hard as she can and runs as many bases as she can until BOTH fielders have touched the ball.

Keep score by counting bases reached before the ball is touched. After all batters have batted, switch sides.

Third to Home

This drill will prepare any player for a game situation when a pop up is hit and the player is on base.

Runners begin on third and break from the base and take approximately 4-5 steps, running in foul territory.

At the coaches' command, the runner tags at third waiting for the coach to give the next command (simulating a fly ball).

At the coaches' command, the runner breaks for home with a slide-by past home plate.

The catcher may want to work on blocking home plate at this time.

Another fun addition is to actually have a coach hit fly balls to the outfield and try to beat the runner home with a throw.

Home to First

This drill is a great simulation of game situations and making quick decisions.

Batters can hit off a tee, bunt or swing the bat and then run to first.

Once the player makes contact with the front edge of the base and look immediately to their right.

The first base coach holds a ball in their right hand. If the coach drops the ball, the runner takes off for second (indicating an overthrow). If coach keeps the ball, the runner turns to their right and returns to first base.

After completing a perfect run to first, the runners stay behind the first base coach waiting for the rest of the team to finish and for the next base running series.

Game

For this drill, you need a softball tee, a ball, and a bat.

You may split the team in half, and should employ one batter and two fielders (from opposing teams) at one time.

Team one has a player at first base, and one at third. Team two has a batter at home plate.

One batter, after hitting, will begin running bases. The closest fielder runs and grabs the ball, and throws it to the other.

The object of the game is to be the faster team.

For each base the batter reaches before both fielders touch the ball, team two gets one point. This drill focuses on speed, for both teams, and has great game simulation.

Resistance

This drill is for conditioning and improving strength in the legs for a stronger lead off when base running.

For this drill, you will need a belt and a piece of durable rope about 10-12 feet long.

A runner wears the belt around his/her waist, with the rope tied onto the back of it. A second player stands behind the runner, holding the rope fairly tightly, so there is little or no slack.

The runner leans forward, while the second player keeps him/her from falling via said rope. The runner should be in sprinting position, with his/her body at a slight 5-10 degree angle. Feet should be shoulder width apart, with the front foot leading by about 6 inches.

When signaled, the runner takes off, with the second player still holding the rope and applying enough resistance to keep the runner in this sprinting position. The runner should make it about 10 yards, rest, and then repeat twice.

Pitching Drills

The W Drill

The "W" drill conditions pitchers in fielding the bunt, making a firm throw, and developing mental toughness.

Draw a large "W" in the dirt.

Stand on the pitching rubber with the "W" facing the pitcher.

The first pitcher throws a pitch to the catcher, drives off the mound to her right, fields a rolled ground ball or bunt from the batter's box, makes a firm throw to first base, and returns to the pitching rubber.

The pitcher then throws her second pitch, drives downhill and fields a rolled ball at the top of the "W", makes a firm throw to second base, then back pedals full speed to the pitching rubber.

The pitcher then throws her third pitch, drives downhill, fields a rolled ball to her left, makes a firm throw to third base, then back pedals full speed to the pitching rubber.

The second pitcher then toes the rubber and starts her round of the same drill, and then the third pitcher, etc.

This drill is to be full speed throughout.

The Noodle Drill

This drill is an effective way to practice stride-foot placement.

The pitcher should be striding across the power line and to the throwing arm side of the noodle, since this is where it is intended for the ball to start.

Hang a rope, string, or preferably a swimming noodle suspended vertically from the ceiling. The noodle or rope should be 5 to 7 feet in front of home plate and as wide as the spot where the pitcher or coach would like the ball to be when it reaches that location.

The pitcher breaks the ball around the noodle. A right handed pitcher will pass the noodle on the right side and, if the ball breaks effectively, she will see the pitch caught on the other side of the noodle.

The Glass of Water Drill

This drill aids the pitcher with an effective visual aid, preventing an early load.

The pitcher holds a glass of water in the pitching hand. A correct pitching motion will allow the glass of water to stay upright until the bottom of the circle, approximately 12 to 18 inches behind the body, as the arm begins to move forward for the wrist snap. At that point the water will spill out of the glass.

An early loader will spill water as soon as she reaches the back side of the top of the circle.

The No Stride Drill

This drill promotes proper ball release and speed when pitching.

The pitcher delivers a ball to a partner without using a forward stride. The partner can be another pitcher for a good warm-up drill.

The stride foot is even with the pivot foot.

The pitcher pitches the ball using good hip rotation, a strong snap of the wrist, and a good follow though, focusing on proper hip and arm mechanics.

Pitchers should be aware of the danger of not rotating the hips and then throwing with only the arm.

The Rope Drill

This drill will encourage the pitcher to stride further.

The coach places a rope in front of the pitcher, about 4 to 5 inches above the ground, at about three quarters the full distance of her stride.

This placement will train her to stride further, and force her to keep the stride leg higher and longer. The distance and height of the rope can be changed gradually, but the pitcher must keep in mind the timing that must occur with the stride foot landing and the arm between ten o'clock and twelve o'clock.

The Chalk Drill

This drill is designed to improve a pitcher's stride aggression.

The coach observes the pitcher's stride on several pitches without the pitcher's knowledge.

The coach then places a chalk mark where her toe is landing and another chalk mark 3 or 4 inches in front of the first.

The pitcher then tries to reach the new mark. If it is easy, repeat another 3 to 4 inches.

Do not try to increase the distance too much in each session.

The Ten Strike Game Drill

This drill helps increase pitching accuracy while adding a bit of fun competition.

This game can be played with two or more pitchers and a catcher.

The object of the game is to throw ten strikes.

The first pitcher throws as many balls as it takes to throw ten called strikes.

The next pitcher tries to beat that number by throwing fewer pitches to get to ten strikes.

The catcher is the judge.

A more challenging game is to count only pitches where the catcher does not have to move her glove to catch the ball. If she moves her glove, the pitch does not count.

The Maxed Out Drill

This drill improves pitchers' accuracy when pitching under conditions in which stamina is being challenged.

Each pitcher works with a catcher. For 30 to 45 seconds, pitcher continuously delivers pitches without any breaks, a speed drill.

The pitcher then takes two shallow breaths followed by one deep breath, releasing tension in the shoulders during each exhalation.

Then the catcher calls a sequence of five specific pitches varied by type and location.

If the pitcher accurately throws the five pitches (judged by the catcher), she has successfully completed the drill.

If not, repeat the entire drill using five different specified pitches.

Repeat until the pitcher has performed this drill 3 to 5 times.

The Four Corners Drill

This drill helps the pitcher develop control and accuracy.

The pitcher throws to the extreme four corners of the strike zone. A catcher or a target on the wall can be used.

When she has achieved accuracy at each spot, she moves the target to the next corner.

To adjust for the in and out targets, the pitcher must adjust her body angle from her normal stance. She turns the toe on the rubber about a half inch in or out from the position she uses to throw to the middle of the plate.

The Side To Side Drill

This drill can be done at home and will help the pitcher become accustomed to various step locations.

The pitcher stands in the middle of a room.

Someone calls out different objects located in different areas in the room - the corner of the coffee table, the lamp, the plant, the left side of the television, etc. - and the pitcher strides toward the object and finishes through the pitch.

This is done, of course, without a ball.

The Striped Ball Drill

This drill helps the pitcher and the catcher visualize rotation the pitcher has put onto the ball.

Draw a stripe right down the middle of the ball.

When throwing a rise ball or a peel drop (straight drop ball) the pitcher and catcher should see a solid line as the ball flies toward the target, indicating correct rotation.

If the line wavers or cannot be seen, the rotation is incorrect and more rotational work is needed.

The straight drop (peel drop) is released off the middle finger and the rotation is clockwise as viewed from third base. If any other rotation is imparted to the ball, the ball will not drop.

The rise ball is just the opposite from the peel drop. The ball must have a counter clockwise rotation as viewed from third base.

The Lateral Reaction Drill

This drill is intended to improve the pitcher's ability to react in a lateral direction to a ball.

Two pitchers work together on the field, one at the defensive position and the other 20 feet in front of the other pitcher with a full ball bucket.

The first pitcher simulates a pitch.

Then the second pitcher throws a ball randomly to the left or right of the pitcher making her reach to catch the ball.

Repeat 10 times, and then the players rotate positions.

The Line Drive Drill

This drill will help the pitcher improve her ability to catch a hard hit line drive and throw to specific bases.

The pitcher pitches a ball which is then caught by the catcher.

As the ball gets near the catcher, the coach hits a second ball as a line drive to the pitcher, who catches it and throws it to second base.

Repeat the sequence with the pitcher throwing to third base.

Repeat the entire drill ten times.

The Bunt Fielding Drill

The purpose of this drill is to train the pitcher to field bunts.

Start with one or more pitchers in the mound area.

Place another pitcher or player at first base and/or second base to receive thrown balls.

The coach tosses a ball from home plate to in front of the mound.

The pitcher fields the bunt using the standard fielding procedure, and throws to first base.

Remind the pitcher to surround the ball by setting her feet toward the base to which she is most likely to throw.

The pitcher then returns to the mound and repeats the bunting procedure, throwing to first or alternating between bases.

The Walk Drill

The purpose of this drill is to build endurance and strengthen the lower body, using it as a generator for her pitching.

The pitcher stands 60 feet away from a partner, also a pitcher, in a grassy area, ball diamond, or gymnasium.

The pitcher takes approximately three walking steps toward her partner before she steps into her pitching motion.

Once in the motion, she throws the ball to her partner, attempting to keep the ball in the air.

She must use her legs and lower body in order to get good lift on the ball.

After she releases, the pitcher takes three steps back to the 60 foot distance.

Once the partner receives the ball, she then performs the same drill back to the original thrower.

Have each pitcher pitch 25 balls.

The 20-4 Drill

The 20-4 drill focuses on strike accuracy and ball control.

The pitcher starts anywhere from one half to her full normal pitching distance, depending on her development and skill.

This drill requires the pitcher to pitch 20 strikes for every 4 balls she pitches. If she pitches the fourth ball before getting the 20th strike, she starts over.

The pitcher should be encouraged to pitch slower, at about 60% of her normal pitching speed, focusing on accuracy.

Be careful to not overwork the pitcher in this drill, because it requires a lot of repetitive pitching, with less downtime between pitches.

The Pitching Distance Drill

This drill is for pitchers needing to improve or practice control and accuracy.

The pitcher starts at half her normal pitching distance from the catcher, and throws a few strikes.

The pitcher then backs up to another designated line, about 10 feet behind the first, throwing a few strikes again.

This continues until the pitcher is throwing from approximately twice the pitcher's normal pitching distance.

The coach can determine how many strikes she must throw before moving on to the next line.

The important point about the pitching distance drill is that the pitcher should essentially keep her form the same as she pitches, regardless of the distance. It is important that she provides the correct amount of power, keeping the body mechanics and pitching technique the same.

As the pitcher moves father out, she should focus on:

- Taking a longer stride

- Making a more controlled final down swing

- Getting a good flick of the wrist at the release

The Dummy Batter Drill

This drill is best for the pitcher who already understands the mechanics of pitching, wants to improve accuracy, and is a great tool for learning new pitches.

The dummy batter drill involves a cardboard or wooden cutout of a batter, standing in her first stance at the plate. The dummy should have a line coming down in front of it, made from a stiff material that will not blow about in the wind.

This line is the proverbial "bulls eye" for the pitcher, providing a visual cue denoting the perfect strike zone.

The dummy batter is great because of the safety concerns with pitching. When a pitcher is learning a new pitch such as the drop, curve, rise, and screw, the batter stays safe and the pitcher is free to experiment as necessary.

The dummy batter can also help the pitcher train for consistency as well.

The Walk Up Drill

This drill helps the pitcher extend her pitching range and get momentum.

The pitcher begins one step behind the mound.

She takes only one step as she presents the ball, then throws the pitch.

The step should be aggressive and long, helping the pitcher to extend her pitching range and gain momentum.

The Circle Speed Drill

This drill improves a pitcher's arm rotation speed, leading to more powerful throws and controlled speed.

For this drill, the pitcher's feet should be wider than shoulder width and in a stride position, as if she has taken a small stride.

The pitcher takes three fast circles with her pitching arm, releasing the ball on the third rotation. The shoulder should stay relaxed but controlled. This is to increase arm rotation speed and to help the pitcher release the ball with more momentum.

To help aim the ball, the pitcher should have her glove hand at shoulder height and facing the catcher, where she intends to throw the ball.

After working on three rotations per pitch, reduce it to two, and then to one rotation per pitch.

The shoulder must be relaxed enough that it can rotate quickly without pain. If the player feels any pain during this drill, she should stop immediately and not attempt to play through the pain.

The Forearm and Wrist Strength Drill

This drill helps increase forearm and wrist strength.

Cut a thick broom handle or a 1" thick dowel to about 2 feet in length. Drill a hole through the center of the dowel, and tie a rope through it. Attach a weight to the other end of the rope.

The pitcher is to hold the dowel with both hands in front of her with arms locked.

She rolls her wrists forward until she has wound up the rope and the weight has reached the dowel.

The pitcher then reverses the motion to unwind the rope until the rope reaches the ground again.

Adjust the weight as she gets stronger.

The Pause and Balance Drill

This drill is effective for the pitcher who "rushes" her motion, falls forward too soon, has trouble getting "on top" of the softball into a high ¾ arm slot, or is imbalanced in the balanced position.

The pitcher starts through her full wind-up without the ball.

When she gets to the balance position, she should stop, hold, turn her head and wait for the coach to hand her the softball.

The coach should vary how quickly he hands her the ball, anywhere between 3-5 seconds.

Once the pitcher has received the ball from her coach from the balance position, she turns her head again and throws to the target, emphasizing a good follow through.

The Weight Training Drill

This drill helps build upper body strength.

Starting with a light weight (4 lb.) dumbbell, do arm curls, butterflies, and wrist snaps in 10 rep sets.

Once the pitcher can do 3 sets of 10 reps, increase the weight starting with 1 set and work up.

Make sure she does not overexert and be certain to consult a doctor before installing a weight program for your pitchers.

The Long Toss Drill

The pitcher takes a bucket of balls and moves to a point just behind the pitcher's rubber.

She pitches a ball that crosses over the plate.

If it crosses the plate, the pitcher moves back 5 feet and throws another pitch.

She continues moving back in 5 feet increments and increasing the arc of the pitch until she cannot get it across the plate anymore.

The pitcher then moves back to the location of the last successful throw and tosses 3 more.

Measure this distance and try to beat that mark at the next practice.

The Broom Drill

This is a drill for young players trying to learn the wrist flip.

Have a fellow player or parent hold a broom horizontally touching the arch in the player's back right where her wrist would hit on the release point.

When she takes her arm behind her and slowly pitches, the pitcher's wrist will hit the broom making her wrist flick the ball.

The coach should remind the pitcher to not throw the ball hard, it should not go far and it will go slowly.

The Pitchers Wall Drill

The purpose of this drill is to train the pitcher to keep her throwing arm vertical.

The pitcher stands with her shoulder next to a wall, approximately 6 inches away from her pitching arm.

Place feet at a 45 degree angle, then go through the motion of pitching the ball.

The Weight Back Drill

This drill trains the pitcher to keep her weight back.

The pitcher delivers her pitch at 75% speed, driving her back knee into her front knee, and holding that balanced position until the catcher returns the ball.

The Timed Snap Drill

This drill builds the pitcher's accuracy.

The pitcher stands 6 feet away from a wall in her stride position.

She throws toward the wall doing only the windmill, not closing her hips.

The ball should come right back to her.

Time her for 15 seconds and see how many she can perform in that time.

Aim to increase the number of pitches with each repeat of the drill.

The Pitching Into Glove Drill

This is a good drill for the pitcher working individually.

The pitcher stands in the stride position with her glove open next to her left thigh.

She follows through to the bent arm position after releasing the ball into her glove.

Many pitches can be practiced with this drill - Wrist Snaps, Pull Downs, "K" Drill, Arm Circle Drill, and full motion.

Use a sock ball or other soft ball to perform this drill indoors.

The Step Back Arm Circle Drill

This drill is for helping the pitcher keep her weight back.

The pitcher stands in her stride position with her glove and hand pointed toward the catcher.

She performs a full arm circle, driving the back knee into the front knee at ball release.

She immediately takes a step back with the back leg giving her a sense of falling back.

Falling back along the power line confirms the pitcher was on balance at the ball release.

The Ball Knee Drill

This drill promotes balance.

Stand in release position.

The pitcher raises her stride knee off the ground (thigh parallel to the ground and calf perpendicular to the ground).

She balances her weight on the pivot leg.

The pitcher then extends her throwing arm over her left thigh and knee, with her glove arm over her throwing arm.

She then pushes her glove arm and throwing arm towards the catcher while pushing out with the stride leg.

The pitcher performs a full arm circle while striding forward, releasing the ball, completing the follow through.

Repeat this drill 15 to 20 times.

The Long Toss Drill

This speed drill works for accuracy while building arm strength.

The pitcher pitches 10 balls from approximately 20 feet.

She then moves back 10 feet and pitches 10 more balls.

Continue until she is as far back as 60 feet.

Once a comfortable accurate distance for the drill has been reached, move to the rubber and throw 20 - 50 hard pitches.

Combining the short and long distances work on both arm strength and accuracy.

The K Pitching Drill

This drill adds power to the pitcher's release and squares the body to the target, increasing consistency.

The pitcher starts out in the "K" position. This is the position the pitcher is in when she has taken her stride toward the plate, glove hand pointing toward the target and the ball hand is at its highest point.

From the third base side, the body resembles the letter "K".

As the pitcher brings her ball hand around toward the release point, she pushes off the pitching rubber with her trail foot violently so it squares the body to the target.

Resources

Over the years I have developed a large network of websites dedicated to Girls Fastpitch Softball.

Some are educational, while some have my softball ecommerce sites.

I thought I would share them with you here.

www.Fastpitch.TV

www.SoftballJunk.com

www.USAfastpitch.com

www.SoftballCoaches.com

www.PitchChart.com

www.iPitch.US

www.SportsDecorating.com

www.WeightedBalls.com

www.Fastpitchmagazine.com

www.BaseballJunk.com

www.Faceguards.com

www.BatTape.com

www.EyeblackStickers.com

www.StrikeZoneMat.com

www.WindmillTrainer.com

www.CatchersZone.com

Conclusion

I hope you found these drills helpful, if you would like to receive my free newsletter sign up at

fastpitch.tv/newsletter

Would you please take a moment to rate it for others on Amazon.com

Best Regards,

Gary Leland

Made in the USA
Las Vegas, NV
30 March 2024

88009475R00066